Cover to Cover
Bible Study

7 Sessions for Homegroup
and Personal Use

1 Corinthians

Growing a Spirit-filled church

Christine Platt

Contents

Introduction

Corinth in Paul's time was a buzzing, cosmopolitan, wealthy city. It was a crossroads for traders and travellers. What was preached at Corinth would quickly make its way to surrounding districts. Paul's evangelistic heart would have skipped a beat at that potential. He stayed for 18 months during his second missionary journey (Acts 18:1–11) in around AD 51–52.

Corinth has been described as the 'New York, Los Angeles and Las Vegas of the ancient world'.[1] This gives a picture of thriving business, higher learning and intellectualism coupled with rife immorality.

The church met in homes, probably in groups of about 30 to 50. This figure is estimated from the excavations of several large houses in Corinth dating from the first century. Maybe one such cell group met in Stephanas' home (1 Cor. 1:16).

The believers were probably from a cross-section of society. In 1 Corinthians 1:26 we read 'not many were influential ... of noble birth', which indicates that some were. Erastus was the city treasurer, and Gaius had a large house where the whole church met (Rom. 16:23).

Paul's letter gives fascinating insights into the life of the Early Church. The believers in Corinth had received 18 months of input from Paul. Later Paul wrote another letter which is now lost (1 Cor. 5:9). The believers then wrote a letter to Paul, and Chloe's people (1:11) came to Paul with a verbal report. So in about AD 54 Paul wrote again and addressed problems of disunity, immorality, lawsuits, prostitution, marriage, Christian freedom, spiritual gifts and resurrection – so many issues had arisen in such a short time!

What was the root of these problems? It seems that some of Paul's teaching had been misunderstood. In enthusiastically embracing the new life in Christ, the Corinthian believers thought they'd 'got it all' and were already living in the Spirit, talking angelic languages and no longer ordinary human beings. They, therefore, felt that the body had no importance: the Spirit was king. This thinking easily led on to two extremes:

- Indulgence/hedonism – they could do what they liked with their bodies, ie prostitution, because the body didn't matter anymore.
- Asceticism/strict self-denial – promoting celibacy, disbelief in bodily resurrection.

The theological term for this is 'over-realised eschatology'. They thought they had received all of God's kingdom now, rather than the biblical picture of experiencing many of God's blessings now, but waiting for heaven for the full package. In layman's terms it's the 'already, but not yet' principle. People of the Corinthian conviction would see no need to grow in their faith as they thought they'd already arrived. Today we might call them triumphalist.

This gives a background for studying this letter, but we also need to keep other important points in mind:

1 Corinthians is not Paul's manual on how to run a church
He was addressing specific questions and situations. For example: 1 Corinthians 7 does not contain Paul's total teaching on marriage. The believers in Corinth had asked him specific questions and Paul had heard of related problems in the church so he gave guidance on these things. If we're looking for Paul's full theological treatise

on marriage, we need to look to his other writings as well
as this letter.

It is a letter addressed to the Corinthian church

That may sound obvious but we need to remember when
we read it that the Corinthian church was encountering
specific and significant problems as they sought to
incarnate Christ in their social context. Our social context
is different. We need to tease out principles from practice
and wrestle with how to apply those principles today
where we are. We cannot blindly apply practices today
which were relevant 2,000 years ago.

Patronage was endemic in the Greco-Roman culture in Corinth

This meant that wealthy influential people gave protection
and help to poorer 'clients', who would in return support
their patron's political ambitions and publicise their good
name. This social norm was totally at odds with Christian
values of servanthood, valuing the weak and promoting
equality among the members. This may well have been
at the root of some of the disunity experienced in the
Corinthian church.

The high value placed on wisdom and eloquence in that culture

The Corinthian believers prized human wisdom and
eloquence in their pre-Christian thinking. With their new
spiritual knowledge they felt they'd reached the summit
of all wisdom, so they looked down on others. They were
impressed with eloquent speakers even if the content
was dodgy. Paul cuts through this with his discussion
on human wisdom and the wisdom of the Spirit (2:13).

Eloquence is of no account unless the cross of Christ is central to the message (2:2). This is a salutary warning for today's Church not to disengage our brains however persuasive a speaker might be.

Even though written 2,000 years ago, Paul's letter is a rich resource for us in the twenty-first century as we seek to 'do church'. We may be surprised or even shocked at the radical nature of Paul's teaching. Our culture exerts huge pressures on us, as the Greco-Roman culture did on the Corinthian church. We are called to be counter-cultural people demonstrating the power of the kingdom of God in our generation. Let's go for it!

Note
1. Gordon D. Fee, *First Corinthians* (Grand Rapids: Eerdmans, 1987), p.3.

WEEK 1

Thank You for the Cross, Lord

Opening Icebreaker

What is your favourite part of going to church?

Bible Readings

- 1 Corinthians 1–2
- John 19:17–30

Opening Our Eyes

The cross and its implications leap out from these two chapters. Paul wants to bring the Corinthians back to the heart of the gospel. This foundation will form the base from which he will address the specific issues facing the church.

First he reaffirms his apostleship as his authority to speak to them (1:1). In verse 2 he states plainly, but in an affirming way, the ethical consequences of being God's people. They are 'sanctified ... and called to be holy'. Paul knows he has hard words to say, so he takes pains to affirm and praise that which is good. They have received grace. God has richly blessed them with spiritual gifts (vv.4–9). This is a constructive pattern to follow in any conflict situation. Even here he sows seeds for teaching which he will pick up later. 'Eagerly wait' for Christ to come (v.7): there is a future component. They don't have it all now (see Introduction).

A multitude of problems faced the Corinthian church and Paul zeroes in on the 'biggie' – disunity. The watching world gazes aghast when Christians can't get along with one another. There were factions in the church. 'Groupies' gathered around different leaders. This was a reflection of the patronage endemic in that culture (see Introduction). Paul's question, 'Is Christ divided?' cuts to the core. Today we live with the legacy of 2,000 years of church – we have endless denominations. 'Is Christ divided?' Surely this has implications for the whole Body of Christ as well as individual fellowships.

Paul's other question, 'Was Paul crucified for you?' reminds us not to put Christian leaders on a pedestal. They are to be respected as leaders but not hero-worshipped. Our focus is to be Christ crucified and risen again.

The cross is the basis of our unity. At its foot is level ground – all are equal in God's sight. We are all unworthy sinners needing forgiveness. There are no super-spiritual Christians.

Although the message of the cross can be easily understood by the least educated or youngest person with an open heart, it doesn't make sense to unbelievers. Paul contrasts human wisdom and spiritual wisdom.

God does things differently from humans. He chooses people the world considers weak or unimportant to reveal His greatness. How many of us have been humbled by a child's faith, or a sick person's joyful spirit? Jesus coming to earth demonstrates this principle. He wasn't born in a palace or into an academic home. The Founder of our faith was born in a stable to an ordinary little family coming from an obscure village. Christian 'celebrities', whether they are entertainers, church leaders or evangelists, need to be especially careful to remain humble before God.

Eloquence impressed the Corinthians. Apollos seems to have scored more highly in this in the Corinthians' eyes than Paul (Acts 18:24–28). Paul turns this on its head by stating that without God's power, eloquence is of no value.

In 1 Corinthians 2:6–16 Paul focuses on the spiritual person. Contrary to the Corinthians' view and possibly to the views of many Christians today, this is not someone with obvious spiritual gifts and possessing wisdom, but someone in whom the Spirit is in the driver's seat. The Christian who kneels at the foot of the cross and is obedient to the Master's voice as relayed to him or her by the Holy Spirit could be said to 'have the mind of Christ' (v.16) – truly a spiritual person.

Discussion Starters

1. How do you think the Corinthians felt when they read 1 Corinthians 1:1–9?

2. What caused the disunity in Corinth?

3. What was Paul's solution to their disunity?

4. What are some issues over which Christians disagree today?

5. How can Paul's solution help with these issues?

6. Why does the cross appear to be foolishness to the world?

7. What difference would it make in your life if the cross was always your central focus? Consider your relationship with God, and relationship with others – Christians and unbelievers.

8. What helps us to keep the cross central?

9. How can we grow in giving the Holy Spirit the driving seat in our lives so as to be truly spiritual people?

Personal Application

The mark of a truly spiritual person is love for others, especially other believers. Jesus said: 'By this all men will know that you are my disciples, if you love one another' (John 13:35). Disunity among believers not only destroys our witness to the watching world, but deeply offends the heart of God. Satan smiles all over his face when he sees Christians tearing each other apart. Are you in a conflict situation? Do all you can to resolve it as soon as possible.

On a more positive note, what can you do to promote unity in your small group, church fellowship, and within the churches in your area? What is a godly way of responding to gossip or criticism?

Seeing Jesus in the Scriptures

Usually crucifixion victims lapsed into unconsciousness through sheer exhaustion before they died. Jesus remained lucid to the end. His final words sounded the death knell for Satan's domination of humanity, and a victorious release for Jesus and God's people. 'It is finished.' Having said that, He emerged as the winner from the titanic struggle against Satan, then bowed His head and died (John 19:30).

In our joy at being people of the resurrection and enjoying all the benefits that Jesus won for us with that cry 'It is finished', let us never forget the horrendous cost of the cross. But let's remember also, that the price has been paid. Our sins are forgiven. None of us should be living with false guilt because 'It is finished'.

WEEK 2

What Should Christian Ministry Look Like?

Opening Icebreaker

If you had to sum up your Christian experience in two or three words, what would you say?

Bible Readings

- 1 Corinthians 3–4
- Mark 10:41–45

Opening Our Eyes

Paul doesn't mince his words. Even though the Corinthians thought they had achieved supersonic spiritual status Paul calls them 'baby Christians' and 'worldly'. The Corinthians allied spirituality with receiving special spiritual insights as individuals, whereas Paul asserts that the true measure of spirituality is displayed corporately in relationships.

The Corinthians' view of ministry was also way off beam. They highly valued eloquence in their Christian leaders. Paul turns this upside down. Ministers are to be servants. For the Corinthians, used to patron/client relationships, this radical turnaround would have sounded crazy.

Ministry is also to be co-operative – one plants, one waters, united in a common task. Neither role is superior to the other. Paul expands on this in chapter 12.

The success of the ministry depends on God, not on specially gifted people … God gives growth (3:6). The work is God's, the field is God's, the building is God's (v.9). He gets all the glory, not human leaders.

Paul has already stressed the centrality of Jesus in 1:1–10. He picks up this theme again by saying that Jesus is also the foundation of the ministry. It follows then that if the ministry is founded on the precious Son of God, what we build on that foundation needs to be of the highest, most durable quality. The *NIV Study Bible* comments on verse 12 this way: 'Gold, silver and costly stones … symbolic of pure Christian doctrine and living. Wood, hay or straw … symbolic of weak, insipid teaching and life.' How tragic to arrive in heaven, see Jesus face to face and realise how much of our time, energy and effort has been poured into activities of no or limited eternal value. Eternal salvation is not in question here, rather the eternal value of the work we do.

On a more encouraging note, even though it seems the Corinthians were definitely Paul's problem child, he still refers to them as God's temple. The 'you' in verse 16 is plural – together they are God's temple. God Himself dwells in them. What a fantastic privilege! But it therefore follows that all their relationships are sacred, special and holy. Paul rightly warns them to treat such relationships with great care!

Paul now responds to the Corinthians' criticism of himself and his ministry style. Rather than defend himself he states that the focus of his attention is not human praise or criticism, but: What does God think of the ministry? Human praise is irrelevant as all gifts, abilities and success are gifts of grace, not of merit (4:7).

Chapter 4:8 is a key verse with regard to over-realised eschatology. They thought they'd got it all and were kings! While Paul confirms that they have received new life, he points to the apostles' experiences of suffering and humiliation to show that the new life is received in its beginnings, not in totality (that comes in heaven). Triumphalism is not a biblical option. As followers of Jesus we need to be prepared to face suffering and shame.

After some fairly harsh words Paul softens his tone. He is their father and they are his dear children. His concern for them forces him to confront their errors. He doesn't wash his hands of them in despair but sends Timothy to help them work through these issues. His example of parental concern is a challenge for us all as we reach out to the world around us, where many societies are characterised by fractured family life.

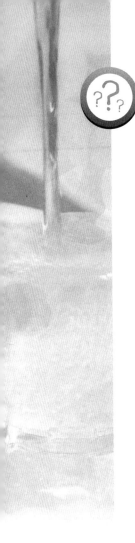

Discussion Starters

1. How does Paul describe a worldly Christian? See also Hebrews 5:11–14.

2. What could you do to help a 'worldly Christian' get back on track?

3. In what ways can a leader demonstrate a servant attitude? See also 1 Peter 5:1–3.

4. Why does Paul emphasise the importance of co-operative ministry?

5. What sort of work comes into the category of gold, silver and costly stones? See also 1 Peter 1:18.

6. How would you respond to someone who was triumphalist or advocating 'name it and claim it' or 'prosperity gospel' teaching?

7. What is a mature godly attitude to suffering? See also 1 Peter 4:12–19.

8. How can we follow Paul's example of having a parental concern for younger Christians?

Personal Application

It is easy to become busy and distracted with all the goodies that twenty-first-century life has to offer. Many of these goodies are positive and fun, but are they the best use of our time and energies? We need to ask the Holy Spirit to help us discern the 'best' from the 'good'. We have a limited lifespan. God urges us to invest it in focused efforts for Him and the extension of His kingdom on earth. Let's not dissipate our energies in anything less than the best.

Take an inventory of your life over the last few months and keep in mind the gold, silver and costly stones analogy that Paul uses. Are there any changes you would make for the future? Make plans to implement these changes as soon as you can.

Seeing Jesus in the Scriptures

Jesus encouraged His followers to invest their lives in 'treasure in heaven that will not be exhausted' (Luke 12:33). In His earthly life He was clearly focused on His purpose and allowed nothing to deflect Him from the path of doing His Father's will. The writer to the Hebrews says it plainly: 'Throw off everything that hinders ... run with perseverance the race marked out for us. Let us fix our eyes on Jesus ... who ... endured the cross ... and sat down at the right hand of the throne of God' (Heb. 12:1–2).

Jesus ran the race marked out for Him. Let's make sure we identify and run the race marked out for each one of us.

WEEK 3

Holy People in an Unholy World

Opening Icebreaker

What is the worst sin you can think of – remembering that all sins are equal in God's eyes?

Bible Readings

- 1 Corinthians 5–7
- 1 Peter 2:4–12

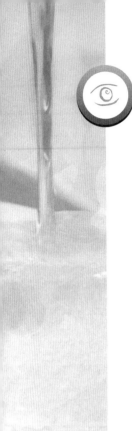

Opening Our Eyes

Sexual immorality and church discipline ch. 5

Paul seems more shocked at the Corinthians' attitude towards this particular sin than he was about the sin itself, even though he views that very gravely. A man in the church had a sexual relationship with his stepmother. The other members apparently not only tolerated this, but looked on with pride. How could this be? Two options have been suggested:

- The man was a wealthy patron and therefore beyond reproach by less influential church members.
- The Corinthians' conviction that they'd 'got it all' and were 'in the Spirit' led them to think they were free to do what they wanted with their bodies. They considered this man was exercising angelic freedom!

The discipline that Paul advocates has the aim of restoring the man (5:4–5). The woman is not mentioned so it could be presumed she was not a church member. Paul's chief concern is for the whole church community (vv.6–8). Sinful behaviour is contagious. If it is tolerated, then others may also be tempted. Christ died to make His Church holy, so believers need to live holy lives.

It seems the Corinthians had misunderstood Paul's earlier letter. When he urged them to separate from sin, they thought that meant to keep apart from all immoral persons including unbelievers. Paul's evangelistic heart was horrified! Christian ghettos are a no-no. Paul warns them against associating with believers who are sexually immoral, greedy, idolaters, slanderers, drunkards or swindlers. Maybe Christians in the Western world need to take a longer look at Paul's words on 'the greedy'.

Keep away from lawyers! 6:1–11

The Roman legal system heavily favoured the wealthy

and influential. Paul is concerned for fairness and equality for all. In an 'I demand my rights'-oriented society, Paul's words in verse 7 hit like a cold shower. 'Why not rather be wronged?' Today's media relishes seeing Christians tearing each other apart in disputes. In such cases genuine God-seekers may turn away, sorrowfully wondering 'Where is God?'

Temples of the Holy Spirit 6:12–20

Not everything Paul writes is his own conviction. Sometimes he quotes what others say as an introduction to presenting his own thoughts. For example, the phrases: 'Everything is permissible for me' (v.12) and 'Food is meant for the stomach and the stomach for food' (v.13, RSV) are considered to be Paul quoting from the Corinthians' letter to him. They thought the body didn't matter. They could eat, drink, have sex as much as they desired. Paul refutes this strongly. Their bodies are temples of the Holy Spirit – therefore holy vessels.

Marriage, divorce, singleness ch. 7

The phrase 'It is good for a man not to marry' is considered to be Paul quoting a Corinthian slogan. He reluctantly agrees in principle, but not with how they are applying it. The ascetic wing of the church advocated no sex in marriage. Paul goes counter-culture in stressing the mutuality of husband and wife. Sexual relations were not the husband's prerogative and the wife's obligation! Both partners 'owned' the other's body. This was radical stuff.

For a more rounded picture of Paul's views on marriage, see Ephesians 5:21–33, Colossians 3:18–19 and Titus 2:4–5. His overall concern here is for Christians to stay as they are – 'bloom where they are planted' – whether married, divorced or single. He elevates neither marriage nor singleness as a more holy state. Both are a gift, given for a certain period of time.

Discussion Starters

1. What discipline does Paul recommend for the immoral church member?

2. Why is it necessary for church leaders to exercise discipline with their members?

3. How should we apply 1 Corinthians 6:7 in a rights-centred culture today?

4. What hope is there for people described in 1 Corinthians 6:9,10?

5. What does 'honour God with your body' mean in practical terms?

6. Singleness has been called the gift that nobody wants. The specific gift of singleness frees the person from sexual desire and longing for marriage and children. How should a Christian, presently single, but without the specific gift of singleness respond to this situation?

7. Increasing divorce statistics indicate much grief and pain. How can the Church help married people stay together and develop stronger marriages?

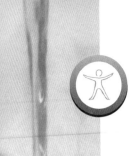

Personal Application

The Church is called to be holy, and every member has personal responsibility to pursue holiness in all areas of life. Those in leadership have an additional responsibility to exercise discipline when necessary. Only when the Church is holy can it have the most profound impact on the watching world. We need to keep our own house in order and not expect the same standards from unbelievers. There is no place for a 'holier than thou' attitude. Our relationships with unbelievers need to be characterised by compassion, and this is costly.

As you've studied this chapter, has the Holy Spirit put His finger on an area of holiness that you need to work on? Bring this to God in prayer. Ask others for help.

Seeing Jesus in the Scriptures

'When they hurled their insults at him, he did not retaliate; when he suffered, he made no threats. Instead, he entrusted himself to him who judges justly' (1 Pet. 2:23). Jesus lived a holy life despite the most extreme provocation. Try to imagine how tempting it would have been to respond to the taunts of the rulers and come down from the cross (Luke 23:35). He could have called legions of angels, shown them who He really was and silenced them forever. But He entrusted Himself to God the Father, knowing that in the end justice would prevail. What a wonderful Saviour and model for us!

WEEK 4

Tightrope Walking

Opening Icebreaker

Which athlete or sportsperson do you most admire and why?

Bible Readings

- 1 Corinthians 8–11:1
- Proverbs 2:1–11

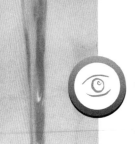

Opening Our Eyes

Ethical decision-making

The Corinthians had asked questions about meat offered to idols. Paul could easily have laid down the law by giving a black-and-white answer. But many questions of life do not easily lend themselves to black-and-white answers. Paul points his readers to overarching principles which will help them determine not only the answer to this question, but answers to other questions which come up. Only in one instance is he categoric – participating in a feast at a heathen temple is clearly wrong (10:21), because this implies worshipping that deity.

For most of us, eating meat offered to idols is a non-issue, but the principles Paul explains will help us manoeuvre through other grey areas. These chapters are about enjoying Christian freedom while maintaining a balance between the permissible and legalism. Sometimes, out of love for others, we need to relinquish our freedom for their benefit, but we also need to cherish our freedom – legalism is an all-too-easy pit for religious groups to fall into.

In chapter 9 Paul gives a practical example. He reminds the Corinthians how he voluntarily relinquished his right to financial support from them in order to not put any obstacle in the way of people coming to Christ. His aim is to do no harm to others' faith while doing all he can to spread the gospel.

We could summarise these chapters by saying that the majority of ethical dilemmas can be answered by a consideration of the following questions:
● What would be of most help to others?
● What would be most beneficial to spreading the gospel?

When considering the possibility of being a stumbling block, it is clear that what is safe for one Christian may not be for another. But Christians are not to be slaves to others' whims and fancies. To be a stumbling block there needs to be a Christian sister or brother who might actually be influenced into sin, not just someone who is offended by one's actions, yet would never be drawn into that sin. These principles can guide us when we consider the types of activities that can lead to sin, but don't have to, such as drinking alcohol, certain kinds of music and dancing, wearing suggestive clothing, playing games that sometimes involve gambling.

We need to relate to unbelievers in order to demonstrate Christ to them, but being out in the world can place us in possibly compromising situations. For example, young people who want to hang out with their non-Christian friends in nightclubs.

Tentmaking
Paul was a tentmaker when he ministered in Corinth (9:12), but in other instances he accepted money from churches (Phil. 4:10–11), though he never demanded it. Being a tentmaker (ie having a paid job while in Christian ministry), has the advantage of giving the person freedom from human strings, while not placing a financial burden on others. Tentmakers are also free from accusation of mismanagement of funds or seeking financial gain from their ministry. Christian workers at home and overseas would do well to consider Paul's model of financial support.

Serious disciple-making
Paul promotes a robust Christianity in 9:24–27, involving discipline, self-control and being focused on the goal. He follows on with warnings from Israel's history showing how a lack of discipline and self-control brought them to ruin. 1 Corinthians 10:13 contains that superb promise of God's strengthening and enabling for the Christian under trial who turns to Him for help.

Discussion Starters

1. What should be the foundation stone of Christian behaviour (8:1–3)?

2. What does Paul mean when he describes some Christians as having weak consciences?

3. What should our attitude be when other Christians criticise our behaviour and we see nothing wrong in it?

4. What should our attitude be towards individuals or groups who are reaching out to unbelievers and experimenting with new ways of outreach that we fear are dangerous or inappropriate?

5. What are the advantages and disadvantages of tentmaking as a missionary model?

6. In what ways is the Christian life like training as an athlete?

7. How would you encourage a Christian who was going through a difficult time of temptation?

Personal Application

Walking tightropes is difficult – one slip sideways and you're gone! Fortunately with Christ we can always pick ourselves up, learn from our mistakes and seek His wisdom for the future.

Is there an area in your life where you've settled for an easy, black-and-white answer when, in fact, you need to exercise more discernment in your opinions and practices? The Corinthians set a good example in that they displayed openness and teachability in asking questions.

Honestly examine your convictions, discuss these with others and be willing to change and grow so as to enjoy your Christian freedom to the fullest while being sensitive to others.

In your relationships with others, has an element of pride about your Christian knowledge and maturity crept in, or are you building others up in love (8:1–3)?

Seeing Jesus in the Scriptures

Jesus didn't shrink from bucking the system. In issues like Sabbath-keeping, washing of hands, attitudes to women, He cut through to the heart of the matter. The legalists hated Him for it. Their security-blanket of rules no longer kept them comfortable and cosy. But the ordinary people loved Him. His teaching blew like a refreshing breeze through the stifling list of regulations they attempted in vain to follow. He brought freedom in every sense of the word – freedom from sin and death, freedom to be ourselves, freedom from self-effort to attain salvation, freedom from fear, freedom to serve, freedom to love, freedom to worship Him.

WEEK 5

Knotty Issues!

Opening Icebreaker

Make a list of all the spiritual gifts and try to identify someone in your group or church who possesses each gift.

Bible Readings

- 1 Corinthians 11–12
- Romans 12:1–8

Opening Our Eyes

Men and women at church 11:2–16

Much hot air has been expended in debating this most complex and controversial passage. One item concerns what men and women should or should not wear on their heads and why.

A timeless principle we can glean is that Christian men should look like men in their cultural context and women should look like women. When Paul wrote, long hair on a man was considered effeminate and short hair on a woman thought mannish, whereas dishevelled hair was common in pagan ecstatic worship. Having her head covered was also a cultural sign of submission to God-given authority. Paul is deeply concerned that Christians should avoid giving any impression of sexual misconduct or idolatrous worship to the non-Christian public. The grounds for his argument are culture-based (vv.13–16). In today's Western world there are no sexual or religious messages in head coverings, although female Christian workers in Muslim lands may decide to wear a veil to be culturally sensitive.

The Lord's Supper 11:17–34

The Lord's Supper in Corinth was celebrated with a shared meal and then the sacrament. This sounds great, but the social climate was such that at dinners the rich and influential received the best food and larger portions. This was the non-Christian norm and it spilled over into the church. Slaves got off work late and the richer church members couldn't be bothered to wait for them to arrive. Paul is blunt: 'You're humiliating the poor! You're causing division! This isn't the Lord's Supper – that's all about unity and caring for the underdog!'

It's interesting to note that there is very little in Scripture to indicate that the Lord's Supper must be celebrated in a certain way. There are no restrictions on who can officiate

or distribute the bread and the wine. A common loaf and
a common cup are symbols of oneness. In *To Corinth
with Love*, Michael Green describes the Lord's Supper in
this helpful way:
* Look back – to Christ's death
* Look in – in self-examination
* Look up – fellowship with God
* Look around – fellowship with each other
* Look forward – to Christ's return
* Look outwards – to proclaim God's Word to others.

Proof of true spirituality 12:1–3
Paul stresses that ecstatic utterings or any other
expression of gifting do not denote true spirituality. This
is demonstrated in a life yielded entirely to God.

Giver and purpose of gifts 12:4–22
Different gifts are given by the one Spirit that we might
serve the one Lord and God. 'Each one' (v.7) is given a
gift. No one is exempt. The newest Christian is gifted.
The gifts are not given on merit or by those who demand
them. The Spirit decides (v.11). The purpose of the gifts is
the 'common good' to serve the Lord and the community,
not self-aggrandisement.

Paul gives a list of gifts, but this is representative, not
exhaustive. He gives other lists (12:28–30; 13:1–3,8;
14:6,26) to help the Corinthians to not overemphasise
prophecy and tongues, but to acknowledge the equal
value of all the gifts.

Unity in diversity 12:12–31a
The major issue facing the Corinthian church was disunity.
Paul uses the powerful image of the interdependence
of the human body to describe how very different parts
(people) must nevertheless live in unity. No part can
function alone. The radical nature of the gospel shatters
human barriers of race, nationality and social status.

Discussion Starters

1. In today's culture, what practical steps can Christians take to avoid giving any impression of sexual misconduct?

2. What practical steps can Christians take to avoid giving any impression of idolatrous worship (making a god of anything in our lives apart from God Himself)?

3. In what ways do you prepare for the Lord's Supper?

4. What should be the Christian's response to the poor?

5. How would you describe someone who is truly spiritual? (12:1–3)

6. How can we make sure we value all the gifts and don't place undue emphasis on any particular gift?

7. How would you help those who think they don't have a gift?

8. What insights can you draw from the image of the physical body as Paul relates it to the spiritual Body – the Church?

9. What can you do, as an individual, or as a small group, to live in the light of being one Body?

Personal Application

We sing 'Jesus is Lord' but do we live it? Try asking your workmates, family and friends: 'From observing my life, who or what do you think is most important to me?' Or in the vernacular, 'Who or what do you think cranks my handle?'

If Jesus is Number One He will be the source of our motivation for living. We will talk of Him and what we're learning about Him and His ways. We will spend time with Him carefully and prayerfully reading His love letter to us (the Bible). The Lord's Supper will become an increasingly special time to concentrate on the wonders and implications of His death and resurrection.

When faced with knotty issues, whether theological or relational, do our thoughts quickly turn to 'What would Jesus do?'

Seeing Jesus in the Scriptures

When Jesus walked this earth He demonstrated the priority of relationship with God. He withdrew from busyness to find a quiet place to pray. He could easily have said to Himself, 'I haven't got long on this earth. I need to give all my time to ministry, preparing my followers to carry on the work after I'm gone. I can't afford to spend time in prayer.'

No matter how pressured He was, He spent time with God. No doubt there were important tasks He didn't accomplish, some sick people He didn't heal, some teaching He didn't fully explain. He may not have met people's expectations, but He completed the work the Father had given Him to do (John 17:4), and that was what mattered.

WEEK 6

Love Conquers All

Opening Icebreaker

Ask each group member to say a few words/phrases in a foreign language. See how many languages you can come up with in your group.

Bible Readings

- 1 Corinthians 13–14
- John 15:9–17

Opening Our Eyes

Without love, gifts are meaningless ch. 13

In this 'love' chapter, Paul puts spiritual gifts in their proper context. The purpose of gifts is to build others up, to do what is best for them, not oneself. The gifts will cease, but love lasts forever.

Are the gifts for now?

Some have interpreted 'perfection' as the end of the apostolic age or the finalising of the biblical canon. This has led them to reject particularly the more 'charismatic' gifts, such as tongues, prophecy, miracles and healings, whereas they may well encourage other gifts, like preaching and teaching. Verses 8–12 do not support either proposition. Also in 1:7 Paul clearly points to spiritual gifts being in evidence until Jesus' return. In addition, Jesus promised the Holy Spirit to all believers forever (John 14:16), and when the Holy Spirit came at Pentecost, He gave gifts to the disciples and subsequently to other believers. This begs the question: Why would the Holy Spirit change tactics when the Church needs all the help it can get? Wouldn't Jesus or Paul have alerted us to such a major change?

Prophecies and tongues ch. 14

The Corinthians' worship services were somewhat chaotic, but Paul does not overreact and instruct them to 'cool it'. He urges them to seek gifts that build up the church as a prelude to stressing the need for intelligibility. Paul's view of worship is that it is participatory, and not a few people on a platform with the rest as spectators. The Corinthians definitely participated, which is a contrast to many churches today.

In *New Testament Prophecy*, David Hill describes Christian prophets as, 'those who have grasped the meaning of Scripture, perceived its powerful relevance to the life of the individual, the Church and society, and declare that meaning fearlessly'. Today's Church needs this gift. However, the words of a prophet are not on an equal footing with Scripture and must always be tested (v.29).

In contrasting prophecy with tongues, Paul affirms his own use of tongues, but categorically declares he would rather 'speak five intelligible words to instruct others than ten thousand words in a tongue'. This perspective may well have shocked the Corinthians, who were somewhat overzealous in their use of tongues.

Paul is concerned about outsiders. The Corinthians could be having a wonderful time of worship by themselves, but if their actions put off the uninitiated, then they needed to stop. He gives clear guidance for tongues messages and prophecies. He wants the worship services to be an expression of: 'God is not a God of disorder but of peace' (v.33).

What about the women?
The most common interpretation of vv.33b–35 is that the Corinthian women were indulging in some form of disruptive speech, which was not contributing to the building up of the church. Paul says this should stop, but he is not giving a blanket prohibition against women's participation in Christian gatherings for all time. This interpretation fits more easily with other passages – Luke 10:41–42, Acts 21:9, Romans 16:1–4 and 1 Corinthians 11:5, where it seems normal practice for women to participate.

Use the gifts wisely
There were excesses in the way the Corinthians used the gifts, but at least they used them. Western rational minds have a tendency to mistrust anything supernatural, but our God is a supernatural Being. If we allow Him full rein He may well shake us from our cosy perch.

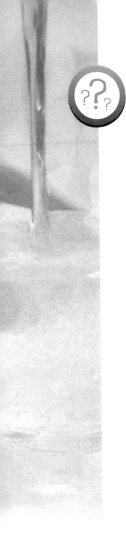

Discussion Starters

1. Why does Paul consider love so important?

2. What is the result of not exercising one's gift in love?

3. Why does Paul commend the gift of prophecy over tongues?

4. How would you encourage someone who thinks he or she has the gift of prophecy?

5. What are Paul's instructions about speaking in tongues in public?

6. What are Paul's instructions about prophecy?

_____

_____

_____

_____

7. What are the implications for church services of 14:33: 'For God is not a God of disorder but of peace'?

_____

_____

_____

_____

8. How would you help someone who is nervous about the gifts of prophecy and tongues?

_____

_____

_____

_____

9. How could you encourage participation in your church services? (14:26)

_____

_____

_____

_____

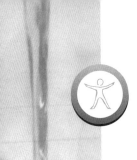

Personal Application

People's experience of prophecy and tongues is varied. Some totally reject them, others go overboard. However, misuse and disuse are equally reprehensible. We need to aim for right use. Where are you on this? Do you need to put aside fear and explore these gifts? Or do you need to rein yourself in and make sure your attitude is always one of love, especially to those who are not of your persuasion?

Our aim should be to honour the Holy Spirit, gratefully receive the gifts He so generously gives us, and use them to the full in God's service. We may need to talk with others, ask for prayer, get a mentor. Wherever we are, God expects us to grow and not remain static.

Seeing Jesus in the Scriptures

In Jesus' last conversation with His disciples (John 13–17) He gave them a new command – to love one another as a witness to the world (John 13:34–35). He went on to promise them the Holy Spirit – the Spirit of truth, the Counsellor whose role was to be with them and to teach them.

After His baptism and temptation, Jesus 'returned to Galilee in the power of the Spirit' (Luke 4:14). He displayed many of the gifts in His earthly life – healings, miracles, teaching, mercy, prophecy. In one of His final prayers to His Father He said: 'I have brought you glory on earth by completing the work you gave me to do' (John 17:4).

May we, in the power of the Holy Spirit, do likewise.

WEEK 7

Marana tha! Come, O Lord!

Opening Icebreaker

Which Bible character are you most looking forward to meeting in heaven and why?

Bible Readings

- 1 Corinthians 15–16
- Revelation 22:12–21

Opening Our Eyes

The resurrection is the pivot on which Christianity stands or falls. If Christ was merely an inspired teacher and role model who died a martyr, Christians are pitiful fools. Why give, serve and suffer for an ideal which has significance only for a short human existence?

Paul based his conviction about the resurrection, first on the historical facts, and second on his own personal experience of the risen Lord. We need to do likewise. Followers of other religions also claim to have a spiritual experience which helps them in life. The Christian's hope is based on the facts of the resurrection as written in God's Word – that Christ was crucified, died, was buried and rose again, being seen by many witnesses, as well as our own experience of Christ as Saviour, Lord and Friend in the here and now.

Will we have bodies or just be spirits floating around in the cosmos? Paul coins this intriguing phrase: 'a spiritual body'. Our new bodies will be fitted for eternity. They will never die or be limited by sin or inadequacy – Hallelujah! Paul backs up his statements by pointing out that God has already made different kinds of bodies – human, animal, fish, moon, stars, so why should it be difficult for Him to give a spiritual body to all of His children?

In Genesis 1 we read about the creative acts of God, and how He pronounced His work to be 'very good'. The full re-creation of our bodies and a world to live in will be a sign to all God's enemies that He has triumphed and His glorious plan has come to perfection.

For those who don't believe in an afterlife, 15:32b is a suitable philosophy to live by: 'Let us eat and drink, for tomorrow we die.' There is evidence of this all around us

– rampant materialism, moral decline, addictions. People search for something to fill the God-shaped vacuum in their hearts, as Pascal described it, but God is spiritual and eternal. All attempts to satisfy inner yearning with anything temporal or worldly are futile and doomed to failure.

Sadly it seems that some Christians also run to the world's goods for satisfaction. But this world is not our home (Heb. 11:16). A quick glance at Paul's life, as well as the lives of other godly men and women, show us that we are not to be too comfortable here, but face our share of hardship and suffering, keeping our eyes fixed firmly on the sure and certain hope of resurrection. The saying goes: 'It's not pie in the sky when you die, but steak on the plate while you wait.' Maybe some of us are focused too much on the steak, rather than the pie.

To encourage his readers, Paul then paints this vivid picture of the stupendous change that will happen at the believers' resurrection – the trumpet will sound, the dead will rise, and we'll get new glorious bodies – death will be dumped in the dustbin!

Paul – the fund-raiser
The Jewish Christians in Jerusalem were impoverished, so Paul sought to raise funds from Gentile churches in Asia and Europe to help them. The Corinthians needed another reminder in 2 Corinthians 8–9, but eventually came up with the goods (Rom. 15:26).

Paul outlines here a model of systematic, regular, self-disciplined generosity in keeping with one's income, plus the need for financial accountability (1 Cor. 16:1–4).

Discussion Starters

1. How does Christianity differ from other religions?

2. What does God promise to believers when they die?

3. What is the fate of unbelievers when they die?

4. How should Christians respond to the truth of the resurrection? (1 Cor. 15:30–32,58).

5. How can we ensure that our focus is on kingdom realities rather than the world and its goods?

Marana tha! Come, O Lord!

WEEK SEVEN

6. What principles does Paul outline concerning financial giving?

7. How does tithing fit with giving according to one's income?

8. In what ways can we reduce general expenditure so as to be able to give more?

9. What can we learn from Paul's experience in 16:8–9?

49

Personal Application

Paul's gut-wrenching cry is *Marana tha!* – Come, O Lord!
How he must have yearned for his struggle, hard work
and sufferings to be over. Jesus' return is closer now than
it was for Paul. Who knows whether He will come in our
lifetime, maybe very soon?

Are you investing all of your life fully for Him? Do you
need to make any changes so as not to be ashamed
when you stand before God and give account of your
life? Think about your attitudes as well as your actions.
Is it your joy to give your all to Jesus? Grasp hold of the
mighty truth of the resurrection. It will give meaning
and significance to any troubles you may encounter, and
enable you to stand firm.

Seeing Jesus in the Scriptures

'Let us fix our eyes on Jesus, the author and perfecter
of our faith, who for the joy set before him endured the
cross, scorning its shame, and sat down at the right hand
of the throne of God' (Heb. 12:2).

The future glory He would experience and the conviction
that His death and resurrection would enable us to share
that glory spurred Jesus on as He faced unimaginable
suffering. He kept His eyes fixed firmly on the goal and
all of His life's decisions were measured against that
plumb line: Would this make the best contribution to
the kingdom? He could have done hundreds more good
things, but He chose to devote Himself to the best. That
takes discernment and courage.

Thank You, Jesus – *Marana tha!*

Leader's Notes

Week 1: Thank You for the Cross, Lord

Aims of the Session
1. To set the scene for a clearer understanding of this letter.
2. To explore some reasons for disunity among Christians and how to address these.

Opening Icebreaker
The aim of this icebreaker is to start off on a positive note. One of the topics of the study is disunity, so it is good to focus on what is positive first of all.

Reading the Introduction to this study guide gives important background to understanding this letter. If your group members haven't read it, give them a few minutes to do that before starting the discussion.

Discussion Starters
1. The Corinthians would have been encouraged by:
- remembering all that God had done for them;
- realising they were part of a bigger organism – the whole Church of God;
- realising Christ was the faithful One who would keep them strong to the end;
- remembering Paul was praying for them.

Some might have been puzzled by 1 Corinthians 1:7–8 if they thought they had it all now. Some might have felt a bit proud of all their spiritual gifts. They might also have felt challenged about being called to be holy as some of them were falling very far short of that.

2. The main cause for disunity in these two chapters appears to be factionalism – people were following

different personalities, rather than having Christ as their focus. People were comparing one leader against another – being positive about one and negative about another.

3. Paul first praises what is good, and then gets them to focus on the cross, not personalities.

4. Christians today disagree on style of worship, preaching, methods of evangelism, the need for social action, the exercise of spiritual gifts, pews/seats, colour schemes, etc.

5. We need to look for and affirm positive aspects in others. Even if we disagree, look for what we can agree on. All parties to a conflict should focus on the cross and remember what Christ has done for us, and that we are equal in His sight. Strive to maintain unity. In grey areas one can agree to disagree, still maintaining essential unity.

6. The world does not have the Spirit of God, therefore cannot understand spiritual truths. Unbelievers do not realise how awful sin is and that the only way for it to be dealt with was for a sinless sacrifice to be made on behalf of sinners. Unbelievers will rationalise sin and think that doing their best is sufficient. For God to die on the cross appears weak to unbelievers.

7. Relationship with God: we would probably be more aware of the awfulness of sin, and more thankful to be forgiven. This would lead to heartfelt worship, and a greater desire for holiness in everyday life.

Relationship with other Christians: a greater desire for unity.

Relationship with unbelievers: more motivated to share our faith.

8. Some ways to keep the cross central are: taking communion regularly, doing specific Bible readings relating to Easter themes, singing worship songs that emphasise the cross, also confessing sin as soon as you're aware of it.

9. This is a day-by-day, moment-by-moment decision to co-operate with the Holy Spirit as He prompts us. Praying through Psalm 139:23,24 gives God the opportunity to reveal blind spots so we can confess sin and remove blockages to the Holy Spirit's action in our lives. Accountable friendships with more mature Christians are helpful as they can challenge our thinking and keep us on the straight and narrow.

Week 2: What should Christian Ministry Look Like?

Aims of the Session
1. To grow in understanding that the Christian life involves serving in love, suffering, possible humiliation, and that our works will be judged by God.
2. To make some practical application.

Opening Icebreaker
The aim of this icebreaker is to break the ice! Also to show that probably most of us would go to the positives – joy, peace, forgiveness, salvation, freedom, new start, etc. – which is great, but suffering and pain are also realities for many.

Discussion Starters

1. A worldly Christian displays jealousy, is quarrelsome, follows human standards in terms of personalities and factions. Paul calls them 'immature baby Christians', uneducated in God's truth.

2. To help a worldy Christian:
- Pray for them.
- Offer to do some discipleship Bible study with them to ground them in the truth. (See Study 1 – remind them that all Christians stand on equal ground at the foot of the cross.)
- Show them 1 Corinthians 3:16–17 ... that disunity, quarrelling and factionalism destroy God's temple, and that is *very* serious.
- Tell them that Christians can 'agree to differ' on grey areas and still maintain the 'unity of the Spirit through the bond of peace' (Eph. 4:3).

3. Ways to demonstrate a servant attitude:
- Eager willingness to carry their responsibilities.
- Availability to those they're responsible for, not just a favoured few (within reason).
- Humble, not arrogant or seeking fame and fortune.
- Appreciating others who also serve.

4. The importance of co-operative ministry:
- We all have a part to play.
- We accomplish so much more together than separately.
- Working together promotes unity. If there are disagreements we need to sort them out so as to be able to continue working together.
- Unity is a demonstration of God to the watching world (John 13:34–35).

5. It is important under this question to make sure group members understand that their eternal salvation is not in question; just the works they have done.

- Faith standing up under trial.
- Obedience to God's Word in all areas – family, work, church, social – living an integrated life with Christ at the centre.
- Loving others.
- Sharing the gospel by word and deed.
- Building up the saved – teaching, encouraging.

6. Response:
- Point them to the example of Jesus' birth, life and death.
- Point them to the experience of the Early Church – Paul and also Peter's teaching (1 Pet. 2:20–24).
- Point them to the present-day experience of many in developing countries – very godly people living in dire circumstances. Also persecuted Christians – living godly lives in prison.

7. A mature, godly attitude to suffering:
- Expect suffering, and don't be surprised by it.
- Accept and endure.
- Respond in love. Don't retaliate.
- Look for what God might be doing through it (James 1:2–4).

Philip Yancey's book *Where is God When it Hurts?* is a valuable resource on this topic.

8. Having a concern for younger Christians:
- Pray for them. (If you don't know any younger Christians ask your youth leader for the names of two or three young people to pray for.)
- Be prepared to open your home and heart to others – step out of comfort zone.
- Set an example for younger Christians to follow.

Week 3: Holy People in an Unholy World

Aim of the Session
To understand that Christians are called to be holy in all areas of life – marital state, relationships within the Church and with those outside of the Church, and to make a practical application in some area of holiness.

Opening Icebreaker
Once everyone has shared, read the list in 6:9,10 and compare. You might want to extend the discussion about being greedy, which tends to be downplayed, at least in the Western world.

Discussion Starters
1. 'Hand this man over to Satan' – this would be by expelling him from the church which would place him in Satan's territory. Being cut off from fellowship with God's people should cause him such grief that he would repent and turn away from sin. This is not so effective in situations where an expelled member could simply walk down the road to another church but discipline still has to be exercised. If an unrepentant church member goes to another church, that church needs to be warned about that person's behaviour.

2. Church leaders have responsibility for the whole flock. If sin is not dealt with, others might be tempted to join them in their sin. The Church is also to be an example to the world of godly living.

3. Christians need to be willing to relinquish their rights in order to display unselfishness. The *NIV Study Bible* says 'completely defeated. Most likely by greed, retaliation and hatred, instead of practising unselfishness, forgiveness and love – even willingness to suffer loss'.

This applies in small matters such as giving way on the roads or in arguments, as well as more weighty matters which might lead to lawsuits. All human lawsuits are of little significance when compared with the Day of Judgment.

However, if one's legal system is fair and just, then seeking justice for others may necessitate legal processes.

4. Paul does not mean an occasional falling into sin, but rather a lifestyle pursued by people who thereby show they do not choose God's way and do not want to enter His kingdom. Some of the Corinthians were rescued out of such sinful lifestyles and were 'washed … sanctified …. justified'. There is always hope for sinners who repent and turn to God – even the greedy!

5. The context is sexual immorality, so Christians should regard their body as a sacred place indwelt by God and, therefore, not allow that body to be demeaned in any way. Being a temple of the Holy Spirit means that the Christian can rely on the Holy Spirit for strength and power to resist sins, such as sexual immorality.

6. Being single, and without the specific gift of singleness, does not absolve the Christian from living a celibate life. What would help would be to focus on the advantages, as in 7:33–35, and also to pray for God's help to live a celibate life for as long as God determines. Accepting God's will is a key to peace.

7. The Church should offer marriage enrichment courses and encourage all married members to attend so that it becomes the norm, rather than marriage courses being perceived to be only for those having difficulties.

Divorce recovery courses are also important. Too often we see people going too quickly from one relationship to another in the hope of finding that perfect soulmate, without dealing with issues arising from the first relationship.

'Preparation for marriage' courses are a vital prerequisite.

Week 4: Tightrope Walking

Aim of the Session
To understand the principles governing ethical decision-making and be equipped to apply these in practice.

Opening Icebreaker
The aim of this icebreaker is to show that hard work, discipline and a clear sense of direction are vital to success in sport – as it is in any aspect of life, including our relationship with Christ.

Discussion Starters
1. Love is the foundation stone, not knowledge. When Christians differ about ethical issues, love should prevail. The Christian should love the brother or sister who has a weak conscience. This is explained further in vv.7–13.

2. A Christian with a weak conscience was one who lacked knowledge and understanding about the meat offered to idols issue. Their consciences were over-scrupulous in terms of Christian freedom. They could not eat meat in faith, therefore to them it became sin (Rom. 14:23). A modern-day equivalent would be a Christian who felt it was wrong to drink alcohol. Scripture forbids getting drunk, but not the drinking of alcohol.

3. We should consider whether this is a stumbling block. Is there a Christian sister or brother who might actually be influenced into sin, not just someone who is offended by one's actions, yet would never be drawn into that sin? Also consider Paul's principles: not to do any harm to others' faith and to do everything possible to spread the gospel.

4. If they are proceeding in faith, then it is between them and God. We need to again consider Paul's principles:
- Not to do any harm to others' faith; and
- to do all he could to spread the gospel.

   A godly response would be to love them and pray for them. One safeguard would be to ensure that they do not go into potentially compromising situations alone, but in groups or teams for mutual support.

5. Advantages:
- Credibility alongside national workers – coping with the same systems they are coping with. One accusation sometimes levelled at missionaries is that they can't get a job in their own country. To counteract this it is important to go overseas with skills and a good employment record.
- The person is not able to be manipulated or pressured by others. In Paul's case, influential patrons may have wanted him to work to their own agenda. He freed himself from any undue influence.
- The cost of sending a family overseas can be huge. Tentmaking may still require some financial assistance, but the burden on home churches is less, so more people can be sent out.
- Tentmakers are often the only ones who can go to 'closed' countries.

Disadvantages:
- Sometimes the amount of time needed to fulfil one's

employment obligations limits the availability of time for ministry to others apart from those in the working environment.

6. An athlete has to train every day. Christians need to be nourished by Christ every day. An athlete is focused and not distracted (Matt. 6:33). Self-control and discipline are daily realities for an athlete. Self-control is a fruit of the Holy Spirit (see also Prov. 5:23). Athletes may not always feel like training, and sometimes we may not feel like getting up early and meeting with God or allowing God's holy fire to penetrate into our souls to expose deep-seated attitudes which need to change. But this is vital for our growth.

7. Encourage them to meditate on 1 Corinthians 10:13 and to look for God's way of escape which He has promised to provide. Pray with them.

Week 5: Knotty Issues!

Aims of the Session
1. To clarify understanding of spiritual gifts and to encourage greater use of them.
2. To explore ways of promoting greater unity within the Body.

Opening Icebreaker
The aim of this icebreaker is to help people know what the gifts are. You could look at the passages noted in the Opening Our Eyes section, and also Romans 12:4–8. A second aim is to help the group recognise how the gifts are expressed. It would be good to make sure the more 'hidden' gifts – such as serving, administration and mercy – are covered.

Note

As indicated in the title, there are several knotty issues in these two chapters, not all of which are able to be covered in a study of this length. If people bring up other questions for discussion, you could encourage them to do extra study. The *NIV Study Bible* has good footnotes and, for a fuller explanation, you could recommend the *NIV Application Commentary on 1 Corinthians*, by Craig Blomberg (Zondervan).

Discussion Starters

1. Some practical steps would involve not wearing provocative clothing, being careful about spending time alone with a member of the opposite sex – even innocent meetings can be misconstrued by unbelievers. Also, being careful about how we touch members of the opposite sex.

2. A self-examination question under this topic could be: What would people say if they were asked to identify what was the most important thing in your life? One should aim for a balanced life with Christ at the centre, and not spend undue time, energy, money or be overly committed to anything apart from God – this would include sport, money, work, pleasure, food, possessions (materialism).

3. Ask God to search one's conscience, using Psalm 139:23,24, and then ask for forgiveness, as well as seek to put relationships right if need be. See also Michael Green's comments in Opening our Eyes.

4. We should share generously what we have been given by God. He expects us to be good stewards (see also Matt. 25:31–46; 2 Cor. 9:6–15). We need to give wisely and ensure that our gifts go to organisations and individuals who are trustworthy. Self-help projects are vital in order to give a 'hand up', not just a 'handout'.

5. Their relationship with Jesus would take precedence. They would talk about what they're learning and experiencing with Him. They would serve others and the Church as they were able. They would use the gifts God had given them. They would display the fruit of the Spirit (Gal. 5:22,23).

6. We need to affirm and appreciate the 'hidden' gifts – administration, serving, mercy. One example is to specifically thank people who serve the coffee and look after babies in the crèche.

7. You could show them 1 Corinthians 12, especially verse 7, and also Romans 12:4–8. You could encourage them to serve … gifts become apparent when they are used. You don't usually discover gifts by sitting quietly in a pew. They should try different avenues of service and then evaluate their experiences with a mentor. They could also go through the worksheet 'Discovering Your Basic Gift', available from CWR (or downloaded free from www.cover2cover.org).

8 and 9. Being one Body:
- Interdependence – all parts are essential even if we can't see their usefulness.
- Strive for unity in our own church, in our locality, and somehow express solidarity with a church/churches overseas.
- Praise God when others are blessed and mourn with those who suffer.
- Celebrate differences in personality, race, culture, age – diversity is a wonderful gift of God.

Week 6: Love Conquers All

Aim of the Session
To explore the gifts of prophecy and tongues and see how they should be used.

Opening Icebreaker
The aim of this icebreaker is to have some fun before delving into these possibly contentious issues. This icebreaker also demonstrates the need for intelligibility.

Note
Some of your group members may have strong views on these issues. It would be good to emphasise at the beginning the importance of love, which includes listening to one another with respect.

Discussion Starters
1. God is love (1 John 4:8). Love is eternal – gifts are temporary. In heaven we will still love, but the gifts will not be necessary. However gifted people are, if they can't act in love, it would be better to not use the gift until they can exercise it in love, however long it takes. The fruit of the Spirit (Gal. 5:22,23) is important as well as gifts.

2. The complete opposite of what is intended – harm rather than edification.

3. Gifts of prophecy and tongues:
   • Prophecy builds the church up.
   • People need to understand what is being said.
   • Tongues build up only the individual, unless they are interpreted.
   • Uninterpreted tongues can put other people off.

4. Encouraging others:

- Pray with and for them – it takes courage to exercise this gift.
- Urge them to talk with a church leader or another person in the church with that gift.
- Make sure they realise that human stuff sometimes gets in the way – so they need a humble, teachable attitude and to check prophecies through with a trusted leader before going public. It's best to say: 'I think this is what the Lord is saying. Please weigh it', rather than, 'Thus says the Lord'.
- Urge them to get a mentor so their gift can flourish as God intends.

5. One, two or three to speak – one at a time and wait for interpretation. This would seem to mean: If there is a tongues message, the worship or service leader should ask for interpretation. If there is no interpretation, no further tongues messages should be brought.

You might want to ask a supplementary question: What case is there for everyone speaking in tongues at the same time? Biblically there seem to be no grounds for this practice.

6. Two or three prophets should speak – one at a time. Others should judge them. 'Others' could be: everyone, other prophets, leaders.

7. Implications:
- Everything should be done in a fitting and orderly way.
- Everyone in submission to others.
- Probably have a leader in overall control, but allowing the Spirit freedom.
- Disruption and disturbance kept to a minimum, ie people not walking in and out too much, young children and babies well provided for in other areas

of the building, mobile phones switched off, people should listen and not chat in the back row.

8. Show them 1 Corinthians 12–14 and Paul's encouragement to be eager to prophesy. Be honest about the possibility of excesses and counterfeit manifestations, but explain that disuse of a gift is as reprehensible as misuse. We need to aim for right use of gifts.

The *NIV Study Bible* says this about the use of tongues as a private prayer language (14:4): 'It is a personal edification in the area of the emotions, of deepening conviction, of fuller commitment and greater love.'

Explain that there is no need to fear what the Holy Spirit gives. He may well shake us out of our comfort zone, but this is the way to growth.

Week 7: *Marana tha!* Come, O Lord!

Opening Icebreaker
The aim of this icebreaker is get people thinking about the incredible future Christians have to look forward to, and also to hopefully create some light relief as some of the material in the study is, of necessity, heavy.

You might need to be sensitive to any members of your group who have unsaved friends and family who have recently died, and for whom they are still grieving.

Aims of the Session
1. To clarify the importance and implications of the resurrection.

2. To make significant life decisions to live in the light of the above truths.

Discussion Starters

1. Christianity differs:
- It is the only one to claim the Founder has risen from the dead and is still alive.
- The only one to claim the Founder is the Son of God, equal with God.
- The only one to offer forgiveness of sins and freedom from guilt.
- The only one to offer salvation by grace alone, not good works, and that salvation is certain, not a 'maybe'.

2. For believers: spirit goes to God, and the body to the ground (Eccl. 12:7). The dead are raised when Jesus returns (John 5:28,29; Rev. 20:11,12). There is the judgment of reward (Matt. 16:27), and then the transformed body with the Lord (Phil. 3:20,21; 1 Cor. 15:49–54), and eternity with God (1 John 5:11,12).

3. For unbelievers: body to ground (Psa. 146:4), spirit to Hades (place of custody, similar to, but not hell itself, to await final judgment – Luke 16:22,23). Rising of the dead, judgment of condemnation, lake of fire (hell – Rev. 20:11–15).

4. Our response:
- Praise!
- Focus should be on kingdom realities, not earthly pleasures.
- Motivation to endure in times of trouble, suffering.
- Motivation to give all in God's service to build up the kingdom, especially in sharing the good news.
- Should have deep abiding peace no matter what the world throws at us.

5. Ensuring our focus is on kingdom realities:
- Regularly reassess priorities in all areas – work, finances, time management, leisure, etc.
- Develop accountable relationship with mature Christian friend or spiritual director to help in assessing priorities, etc.
- Regularly ask oneself the question: If today were my last day on earth, how would I invest it?

6. The principles are: be systematic, regular, self-disciplined, give in keeping with your income – therefore needs reassessing when your income goes up or down. The importance and responsibility of meeting the needs of the poor.

7. Tithing is an Old Testament principle that Jesus affirms in Matthew 23:23 and Luke 11:42. The New Testament tends to stress 'in keeping with one's income'. So 10 per cent may be too much for those on a low income, but too little for those on higher incomes (cf. 2 Cor. 8–9).

8. Some practical ideas are: using less water and power. Recycling, regularly giving away unused clothes, toys, books, etc. Down-sizing in homes and cars, eating less, eating out less, having fewer clothes, spending less money on pets, having more modest weddings and funerals, giving donations to Christian ministries as Christmas and birthday presents, limiting window shopping or watching TV ads – this encourages us to buy more, especially stuff we don't need.

9. Open doors for ministry and opposition often go hand in hand. If there is no open door for a long time, that might mean it's a closed door, and if there is never any opposition, it might mean looking to see if the true gospel is being preached.

NATIONAL DISTRIBUTORS

UK: (and countries not listed below)

CWR, Waverley Abbey House, Waverley Lane, Farnham, Surrey GU9 8EP.
Tel: (01252) 784700 Outside UK (44) 1252 784700 Email: mail@cwr.org.uk

AUSTRALIA: KI Entertainment, Unit 21 317-321 Woodpark Road, Smithfield, New South Wales 2164.
Tel: 1 800 850 777 Fax: 02 9604 3699 Email: sales@kientertainment.com.au

CANADA: David C Cook Distribution Canada, PO Box 98, 55 Woodslee Avenue, Paris, Ontario N3L 3E5.
Tel: 1800 263 2664 Email: swansons@cook.ca

GHANA: Challenge Enterprises of Ghana, PO Box 5723, Accra.
Tel: (021) 222437/223249 Fax: (021) 226227 Email: ceg@africaonline.com.gh

HONG KONG: Cross Communications Ltd, 1/F, 562A Nathan Road, Kowloon.
Tel: 2780 1188 Fax: 2770 6229 Email: cross@crosshk.com

INDIA: Crystal Communications, 10-3-18/4/1, East Marredpalli, Secunderabad – 500026, Andhra Pradesh.
Tel/Fax: (040) 27737145 Email: crystal_edwj@rediffmail.com

KENYA: Keswick Books and Gifts Ltd, PO Box 10242-00400, Nairobi.
Tel: (254) 20 312639/3870125 Email: keswick@swiftkenya.com

MALAYSIA: Salvation Book Centre (M) Sdn Bhd, 23 Jalan SS 2/64, 47300 Petaling Jaya, Selangor.
Tel: (03) 78766411/78766797 Fax: (03) 78757066/78756360 Email: info@salvationbookcentre.com

Canaanland, No. 25 Jalan PJU 1A/41B, NZX Commercial Centre, Ara Jaya, 47301 Petaling Jaya, Selangor.
Tel: (03) 7885 0540/1/2 Fax: (03) 7885 0545 Email: info@canaanland.com.my

NEW ZEALAND: KI Entertainment, Unit 21 317-321 Woodpark Road, Smithfield, New South Wales 2164, Australia.
Tel: 0 800 850 777 Fax: +612 9604 3699 Email: sales@kientertainment.com.au

NIGERIA: FBFM, Helen Baugh House, 96 St Finbarr's College Road, Akoka, Lagos.
Tel: (01) 7747429/4700218/825775/827264 Email: fbfm@hyperia.com

PHILIPPINES: OMF Literature Inc, 776 Boni Avenue, Mandaluyong City.
Tel: (02) 531 2183 Fax: (02) 531 1960 Email: gloadlaon@omflit.com

SINGAPORE: Alby Commercial Enterprises Pte Ltd, 95 Kallang Avenue #04-00, AIS Industrial Building, 339420.
Tel: (65) 629 27238 Fax: (65) 629 27235 Email: marketing@alby.com.sg

SOUTH AFRICA: Struik Christian Books, 80 MacKenzie Street, PO Box 1144, Cape Town 8000.
Tel: (021) 462 4360 Fax: (021) 461 3612 Email: info@struikchristianmedia.co.za

SRI LANKA: Christombu Publications (Pvt) Ltd, Bartleet House, 65 Braybrooke Place, Colombo 2.
Tel: (9411) 2421073/2447665 Email: dhanad@bartleet.com

USA: David C Cook Distribution Canada, PO Box 98, 55 Woodslee Avenue, Paris, Ontario N3L 3E5, Canada. Tel: 1800 263 2664 Email: swansons@cook.ca

CWR is a Registered Charity - Number 294387
CWR is a Limited Company registered in England - Registration Number 1990308

Day and Residential Courses
Counselling Training
Leadership Development
Biblical Study Courses
Regional Seminars
Ministry to Women
Daily Devotionals
Books and DVDs
Conference Centre

Trusted all Over the World

CWR HAS GAINED A WORLDWIDE reputation as a centre of excellence for Bible-based training and resources. From our headquarters at Waverley Abbey House, Farnham, England, we have been serving God's people for over 40 years with a vision to help apply God's Word to everyday life and relationships. The daily devotional *Every Day with Jesus* is read by nearly a million people in more than 150 countries, and our unique courses in biblical studies and pastoral care are respected all over the world. Waverley Abbey House provides a conference centre in a tranquil setting.

For free brochures on our seminars and courses, conference facilities, or a catalogue of CWR resources, please contact us at the following address.
CWR, Waverley Abbey House, Waverley Lane, Farnham, Surrey GU9 8EP, UK

Telephone: **+44 (0)1252 784700**
Email: mail@cwr.org.uk
Website: www.cwr.org.uk

CWR Applying God's Word
to everyday life and relationships

Dramatic new resources

2 Corinthians: Restoring harmony
by Christine Platt

Paul's message went against the grain of the culture in Corinth, and even his humility was in stark contrast to Greco–Roman culture. Be challenged and inspired to endure suffering, seek reconciliation, pursue holiness and much more as you look at this moving letter which reveals Paul's heart as much as his doctrine. This thought-provoking, seven-week study guide is great for individual or small-group use.
ISBN: 978-1-85345-551-3

Isaiah 40–66: Prophet of restoration
by John Houghton

God is a God of new beginnings, a God of second chances who takes no pleasure in punishment. However, profound lessons must be learned if the same errors are to be avoided in the future. Understand Isaiah's powerful message for each of us, that God is a holy God who cannot ignore sin, but One who also displays amazing grace and mercy, and who longs to enjoy restored relationship with us. These seven inspiring and challenging studies are perfect for individual or small-group use.
ISBN: 978-1-85345-550-6

Also available in the bestselling
Cover to Cover Bible Study Series

1 Corinthians
Growing a Spirit-filled church
ISBN: 978-1-85345-374-8

Fruit of the Spirit
Growing more like Jesus
ISBN: 978-1-85345-375-5

1 Timothy
Healthy churches – effective Christians
ISBN: 978-1-85345-291-8

Genesis 1–11
Foundations of reality
ISBN: 978-1-85345-404-2

23rd Psalm
The Lord is my shepherd
ISBN: 978-1-85345-449-3

God's Rescue Plan
Finding God's fingerprints on human histc
ISBN: 978-1-85345-294-9

2 Timothy and Titus
Vital Christianity
ISBN: 978-1-85345-338-0

Great Prayers of the Bible
Applying them to our lives today
ISBN: 978-1-85345-253-6

Ecclesiastes
Hard questions and spiritual answers
ISBN: 978-1-85345-371-7

Hebrews
Jesus – simply the best
ISBN: 978-1-85345-337-3

Ephesians
Claiming your inheritance
ISBN: 978-1-85345-229-1

Hosea
The love that never fails
ISBN: 978-1-85345-290-1

Esther
For such a time as this
ISBN: 978-1-85345-511-7

Isaiah 1–39
Prophet to the nations
ISBN: 978-1-85345-510-0

James
Faith in action
ISBN: 978-1-85345-293-2

Jeremiah
The passionate prophet
ISBN: 978-1-85345-372-4

Joseph
The power of forgiveness and reconciliation
ISBN: 978-1-85345-252-9

Mark
Life as it is meant to be lived
ISBN: 978-1-85345-233-8

Moses
Face to face with God
ISBN: 978-1-85345-336-6

Nehemiah
Principles for life
ISBN: 978-1-85345-335-9

Parables
Communicating God on earth
ISBN: 978-1-85345-340-3

Philemon
From slavery to freedom
ISBN: 978-1-85345-453-0

Philippians
Living for the sake of the gospel
ISBN: 978-1-85345-421-9

Proverbs
Living a life of wisdom
ISBN: 978-1-85345-373-1

Revelation 1–3
Christ's call to the Church
ISBN: 978-1-85345-461-5

Revelation 4–22
The Lamb wins! Christ's final victory
ISBN: 978-1-85345-411-0

Rivers of Justice
Responding to God's call to righteousness today
ISBN: 978-1-85345-339-7

Ruth
Loving kindness in action
ISBN: 978-1-85345-231-4

The Covenants
God's promises and their relevance today
ISBN: 978-1-85345-255-0

The Divine Blueprint
God's extraordinary power in ordinary lives
ISBN: 978-1-85345-292-5

The Holy Spirit
Understanding and experiencing Him
ISBN: 978-1-85345-254-3

The Image of God
His attributes and character
ISBN: 978-1-85345-228-4

The Kingdom
Studies from Matthew's Gospel
ISBN: 978-1-85345-251-2

The Letter to the Colossians
In Christ alone
ISBN: 978-1-85345-405-9

The Letter to the Romans
Good news for everyone
ISBN: 978-1-85345-250-5

The Lord's Prayer
Praying Jesus' way
ISBN: 978-1-85345-460-8

The Prodigal Son
Amazing grace
ISBN: 978-1-85345-412-7

The Second Coming
Living in the light of Jesus' return
ISBN: 978-1-85345-422-6

The Sermon on the Mount
Life within the new covenant
ISBN: 978-1-85345-370-0

The Tabernacle
Entering into God's presence
ISBN: 978-1-85345-230-7

The Uniqueness of our Faith
What makes Christianity distinctive?
ISBN: 978-1-85345-232-1

£3.99 each (plus p&p)
Price correct at time of printing

Cover to Cover Every Day
Gain deeper knowledge of the Bible

Each issue of these bimonthly daily Bible-reading notes gives you insightful commentary on a book of the Old and New Testaments with reflections on a psalm each weekend by Philip Greenslade.

Enjoy contributions from two well-known authors every two months, and over a five-year period you will be taken through the entire Bible.

ISSN: 1744-0114
Only £2.49 each (plus p&p)
£13.80 for annual UK subscription (6 issues)
£13.80 for annual email subscription
(available from www.cwr.org.uk/store)